Roman Provinces

0   200   400   600   800   1000 k

0   100   200   300   400   500   600 mi

D0835589

PARTHIAN
EMPIRE

ARMENIA

BITHYNIA-
PONTUS

Philippi
42BC

MACEDONIA

ASIA

Actium
31BC

CILICIA

Tarsus

Ephesus

Athens

Antioch

ACHAIA

SYRIA

CYPRUS

CRETE

JUDAEA

MEDITERRANEAN SEA

Alexandria

CYRENAICA

Memphis

EGYPT

River
Nile

Thebes

RED SEA

WHO WAS
CLEOPATRA?

GERALDINE HARRIS

ILLUSTRATED BY PETER DENNIS

First published in Great Britain 1997 by
Macdonald Young Books an imprint of
Wayland Books Ltd
61 Western Road
Hove
East Sussex BN3 1JD

Find Wayland on the internet at:
http://www.wayland.co.uk

Series concept and text
© Wendy and Sally Knowles

Design and illustrations
© Macdonald Young Books

Edited by Wendy Knowles
Designed by David Fordham

Printed and bound in
Typeset by Stylize

ISBN 07500 2270 1

The front-cover portrait of Cleopatra is
based on coins and statues from her reign.
As Cleopatra came from a Greek family,
she mainly wore Greek hairstyles and
jewellery.

Photograph acknowledgements:

We are grateful to the following for permission
to reproduce photographs:
Front cover: The British Museum, London, (br);
Peter Clayton, (tl); Michael Holford (tr and bl);

American Numismatic Society, page 12;
Bildarchiv Preussischer Kulturbesitz, page
14(l), 21(bc) (Aufn G. Stenze); The Bridgeman
Art Library, London/Lauros-Giraudon,
page 9(r); The Bridgeman Art Library,
London/Giraudon, page 16, The Bridgeman
Art Library,London/Louvre, Paris, page 22(r);
City of Bristol Museum & Art Gallery, Dept. of
Archaeology, page 25(tr); The British Museum,
London, pages 8, 18(l), 26(l), 28(l), 31(t), 32,
33(t), 36(r), 41; The Brooklyn Museum,
Charles Edwin Wilbour Fund, page 39(r);
Peter Clayton, pages 9(l), 11, 18(r), 19, 21(r),
27, 31(b), 33(b), 34(r), 37, 40(l), 40(r); Michael
Holford, pages 10(b), 14(r), 15(t), 15(b), 17(t),
17(b), 22(l), 28(r); The Louvre, Paris/RMN,
pages 10(t) (Hervé Lewandowski), 13, 25(b), 30
(Arnaudet), 36(l); The Museum of Fine Arts,
Houston, page 39(l); National Trust
Photographic Library, page 21(l) (Paul
Mulcahy); G. Pinch, page 26(r); Ronald
Sheridan/Ancient Art & Architecture
Collection, pages 25(tl), 35; Vatican Museums,
page 34(l).

Picture Research by Valerie Mulcahy

CONTENTS

CLEOPATRA'S EGYPT

Cleopatra is one of the most famous women who ever lived. She ruled Egypt for 21 years in the 1st century BC. She was the seventh queen of Egypt of that name. Her family were Greeks from Macedonia.

HOW DID A GREEK FAMILY COME TO BE RULING EGYPT?

For thousands of years Egypt was ruled by Egyptian kings known as Pharaohs. Then in the 4th century BC, the young King of Macedonia, Alexander the Great, conquered Egypt and most of the near East. When he died, his vast empire began to break up. One of Alexander's generals, a man named Ptolemy, made himself King of Egypt. His family are known as the Ptolemies. They ruled Egypt for about 300 years. In the 3rd century BC, the Ptolemies conquered Cyprus and parts of what are now Turkey, Lebanon, Israel and Libya. They ruled from a great city called Alexandria.

Glass square (above), inlaid with a mosaic glass eye of the Egyptian god, Horus. A type of decorative glass popular in Cleopatra's time.

Portrait of Cleopatra (left). As Cleopatra came from a Greek family, she mainly wore Greek hairstyles and jewellery.

WHAT WAS SPECIAL ABOUT ALEXANDRIA?

One of the most important ports on the Mediterranean it was famous for two things: its large lighthouse and its library. The great library had more books than had ever been collected in one place before. Scholars came from all over the Greek world to study in the library, and in the Museum (*university*) next to the royal palace. People of many different races lived in Alexandria. It was a violent place and the citizens often rioted against their rulers.

Portrait of Alexander the Great (right), who conquered Egypt and founded the city of Alexandria.

Coin showing the Pharos lighthouse (above), one of the Seven Wonders of the ancient world. The lighthouse is thought to have been about 150 metres high.

WERE THE PTOLEMIES POPULAR RULERS?

The native Egyptians were not happy about being ruled by Greeks. There were often rebellions in the south of Egypt. The Ptolemies were a quarrelsome family. Egypt lost most of its empire while the later Ptolemies were fighting and murdering each other. During these civil wars some of the kings made the mistake of asking for help from the strongest people in Europe – the Romans.

WHY WAS ROME A THREAT TO EGYPT?

Egypt was the richest country in the ancient world. The fertile soil of the Nile Valley could grow several crops a year. Gold and precious gems were mined in the Egyptian deserts. The Romans needed gold to pay their armies and grain to feed them. Rome's ultimate aim was to make Egypt part of its growing empire. All her life, Cleopatra fought hard to prevent this from happening.

CLEOPATRA'S CHILDHOOD

Cleopatra was born at a troubled time in Egypt's history. Her father only came to the throne because the previous king, who had murdered his wife, had in his turn, been murdered by an angry mob after ruling for just 19 days.

Portrait of Cleopatra's father, King Ptolemy 12. His nickname was Ptolemy the Flute Player.

WHO WERE HER PARENTS?

Her father was King Ptolemy 12. Her mother was a princess called Cleopatra Tryphania, who was either her father's full or half-sister. Her mother probably died shortly after Cleopatra's birth and Ptolemy 12 married again. We don't know how Cleopatra felt about her step-mother, but she seems to have been very fond of her father. When she became queen she took the title of 'Father-loving Goddess'.

It was the custom for Egyptian kings to marry their sisters. Doing things that ordinary people weren't allowed to do made the royal family seem more like gods.

This pull-along wooden horse (below), is the kind of toy that Cleopatra and her brothers and sisters might have played with.

DID SHE HAVE ANY BROTHERS OR SISTERS?

Cleopatra probably had two older sisters – the proud Princess Bernice and another sister called Cleopatra. Ptolemy 12 also had three children by his second wife: a girl, Arsinoe, and two boys, both called Ptolemy. It was not a happy family. The children all thought of each other as rivals for the throne.

Cleopatra would have been taught in the palace by tutors. Each prince or princess had a foster-father who was in charge of their education. Cleopatra would have been taught maths, Greek literature, public speaking and philosophy. She was the first of her family to learn the native Egyptian language. Even her enemies agreed that she was very clever. She is said to have spoken at least eight languages and to have been a great reader.

Schoolchild's writing board (above), from Egypt, with lines from a famous Greek poem, Homer's Illiad.

Cleopatra would have spoken Greek at home. She was the first of her family to learn the native Egyptian language.

The young Cleopatra dances to please her father and the gods.

A FAMILY AT WAR

Ptolemy 12 dreamed of rebuilding the empire of Alexander, but he was not a strong ruler. He raised taxes to send huge bribes to the two most powerful men in Rome, Cnaeus Pompey and Julius Caesar. In return, he was made an official 'Friend' of Rome. Soon afterwards the Romans seized Cyprus, which was ruled by Ptolemy 12's brother. The people of Alexandria felt that Ptolemy 12 had betrayed his brother and his country. There were riots and the king fled to Rome.

Coin of Cleopatra's father (above), Ptolemy 12. Coins weren't used in Egypt until the 4th century BC.

Cleopatra and her brother Ptolemy 13 are crowned co-rulers of Egypt.

WHO RULED EGYPT NEXT?

Egypt was now ruled by Cleopatra's two older sisters, Cleopatra 6 and Bernice. After Cleopatra 6's death, Bernice seized power for herself. She needed a husband, because the Egyptians liked to be ruled by a queen and a king. She married a Greek prince from Syria. He turned out to be a coarse young man with an unpleasant smell. Bernice couldn't stand him and after just three days she had him strangled. She liked her next husband, Archelaus, much better.

HOW DID CLEOPATRA COME TO BE QUEEN?

Ptolemy 12 managed to bribe a Roman general into lending him an army. Some of these troops were led by a brilliant young soldier called Mark Antony. He invaded Egypt and defeated Bernice. It was here that he met Cleopatra for the first time. When Ptolemy 12 was back in power he had Bernice put to death. Cleopatra would have been about 14 when this happened. It must have taught her that a Ptolemy had to be ruthless to survive. After Ptolemy 12 died, Cleopatra, aged 18, was made Queen of Egypt, with her 10 year-old half-brother, Ptolemy 13 as her husband and co-ruler.

Here, Cleopatra is shown as an Egyptian pharaoh making offerings to the Egyptian goddess Isis. It is very unlikely that Cleopatra ever dressed this way in real life.

In Cleopatra's family, the women tended to be cleverer and more ambitious than the men. All of Ptolemy 12's daughters wanted to rule Egypt.

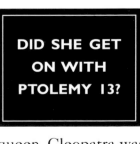

DID SHE GET ON WITH PTOLEMY 13?

No. He had a Regency Council to help him rule. They didn't like sharing power with Cleopatra, and her half-sister, Arsinoe, wanted to be queen. Cleopatra was soon driven out of the country. It looked as though her reign was over.

THE REAL CLEOPATRA

Poets have written about the fabulous beauty of Cleopatra for 2,000 years, but some of the coins that date from her reign make her look quite ugly. The Greek historian, Plutarch, tells us that Cleopatra was not particularly beautiful, but it was her wit and charm that made her so irresistable.

WHAT DID SHE REALLY LOOK LIKE?

It is possible that Cleopatra had an Egyptian or Syrian grandmother, but the rest of her family were Greek, so she probably wouldn't have been very dark-skinned. It's likely that she had dark brown hair, although some Greeks from Macedonia had red or blonde hair. To judge from her statues, she had large eyes, a full mouth and a long elegant nose.

WHAT SORT OF CLOTHES DID SHE WEAR?

Cleopatra usually dressed in Greek rather than Egyptian style. Greek women wore a draped length of material, rather like an Indian sari, over a long undertunic. The Roman poet Lucan describes Cleopatra wearing a dress of silk so fine that her white body shone through it.

This beautiful head (left), is thought to be a portrait of Cleopatra. The hair was once painted a reddish-brown.

Gold dove earrings (below). Doves were the symbol of Aphrodite, the Greek goddess of love and beauty.

'CLEOPATRA'S CURE' FOR THINNING HAIR
*R*ub the scalp with a mixture of honey, bear-grease and burnt mice!

Greek kings and queens wore gold diadems or crowns like this one.

DID SHE REALLY BATHE IN MILK?

Cleopatra may have bathed in the milk of asses to keep herself looking young and beautiful. Women in Egypt used all kinds of fats to stop their skin getting sunburnt. A sparkling black powder called kohl was used as an eye-liner to protect the eyes against the glare of the sun. Cleopatra would also have used green eyeshadow made from malachite. She probably coloured her lips with ochre and her fingernails with a vegetable dye called henna.

Cleopatra's favourite servants, Iras and Charmian, do her hair and make-up.

Glass perfume bottle (left). Egypt was famous for its perfumes.

CLEOPATRA AND JULIUS CAESAR

Ptolemy 13 was ruling in Alexandria with the help of the Regency Council and his sister, Arsinoe. Meanwhile a civil war was going on in Rome between the two great Roman generals, Julius Caesar and Cnaeus Pompey. When Pompey arrived in Egypt to ask for help he was murdered on the orders of the Regency Council. Caesar arrived in Alexandria three days later in pursuit of Pompey. It was here that he met Cleopatra for the first time.

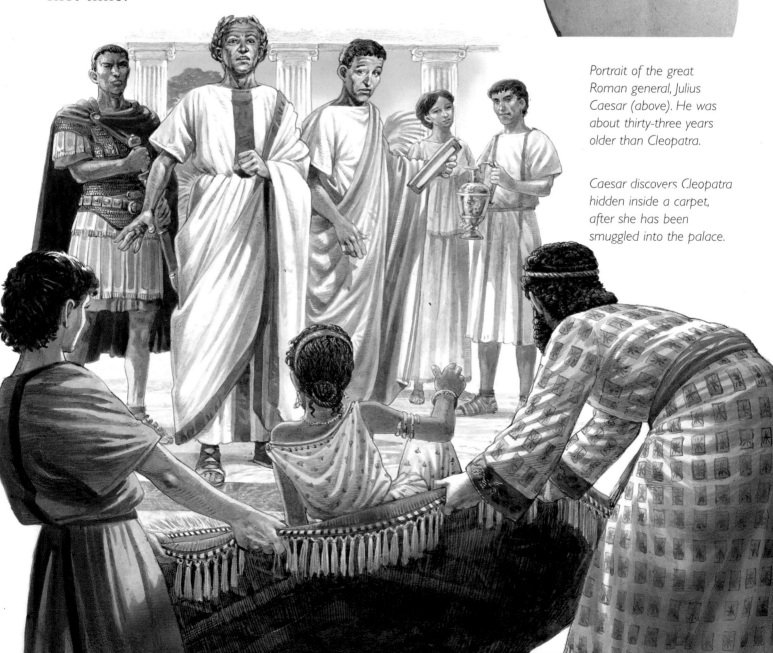

Portrait of the great Roman general, Julius Caesar (above). He was about thirty-three years older than Cleopatra.

Caesar discovers Cleopatra hidden inside a carpet, after she has been smuggled into the palace.

HOW DID CLEOPATRA AND CAESAR MEET?

Cleopatra wanted Caesar to make her queen again, but she was afraid that her brother would murder her before she could meet Caesar and get his support. So she sailed to Alexandria on the ship of a friendly merchant. He wrapped her up in a carpet and carried this into the palace as a present for Caesar. Caesar admired Cleopatra's courage and was soon won over by her charm and intelligence. He insisted that the Egyptians make her queen again.

Coin of Julius Caesar. He was the first Roman leader to be shown on coins during his own lifetime.

WAS PTOLEMY 13 PLEASED?

He was so cross that he threw his crown onto the floor! Caesar thought that he had settled everything peacefully, but the Regency Council were plotting to kill him. Caesar soon found himself under siege in the royal palace by an army led by Arsinoe. At one point in a battle in the harbour he even had to swim for his life.

HOW DID THE WAR END?

When troops loyal to Caesar finally arrived, he sailed along the coast to meet them. A great battle was fought against the Egyptian army. The Egyptians were defeated and Arsinoe was captured. Ptolemy 13 tried to escape in a boat, but he was weighed down by his gold armour and drowned. Caesar made Cleopatra Queen of Egypt and Cyprus, but she had to have her youngest half-brother, Ptolemy 14, as her co-ruler.

Roman mosaic showing the River Nile. Cleopatra and Caesar celebrated their victory with a cruise along the Nile.

CLEOPATRA IN ROME

Caesar soon had to leave Egypt, but he left Roman troops to protect Cleopatra. A few months after he returned to Rome, Cleopatra had a baby. It was a boy and she called him Ptolemy Caesarion.

WAS CAESARION JULIUS CAESAR'S SON?

Cleopatra thought of Caesar as her husband. Kings of Egypt had always been allowed more than one wife, so the fact that Caesar was already married didn't trouble her. Caesar's three marriages had only produced one daughter. He was now 52 years old and in poor health. Caesar himself clearly believed that Caesarion was his only son. He invited Cleopatra and her family to Rome. There she would have met Mark Antony again, who was now Caesar's second-in-command.

Coin from Cyprus (above), showing Cleopatra with her baby son, Caesarion.

Cleopatra and her son Caesarion on the back wall of the temple of Dendera (right). She is dressed as an Egyptian goddess.

WHY DID CAESAR INVITE CLEOPATRA TO ROME?

Caesar just seems to have enjoyed her company more than that of any other woman. He set up a golden statue of her in the new temple he had built for Venus, the Roman goddess of love. He also gave her the special status of 'Friend of Rome'. As long as he lived Egypt was safe from Roman aggression. But he had many enemies.

WAS SHE A CAUSE OF HIS UNPOPULARITY?

Supporters of the old Roman Republic thought Caesar, who was now Dictator, had too much power. They were also horrified to think that Caesar might actually marry a foreigner like Cleopatra and make her son his heir.

*Head of Caesar (right).
He had become
Dictator of Rome, but
he had many enemies.*

WHAT HAPPENED TO CAESAR?

The people who wanted to restore the Republic decided that Caesar must die. The leaders of the plot to kill him were Cassius, and Marcus Brutus, whom Caesar had always treated like a son. The plotters surrounded Caesar in the Senate House and stabbed him to death. This must have been a terrible shock for Cleopatra. She and her family hurriedly left Rome. Cleopatra soon had to forget her grief for Caesar. To keep Egypt free, she needed to make an alliance with the new leaders of Rome.

*Cleopatra and her family
hear the terrible news of
Caesar's murder.*

MARK ANTONY

Caesar's murderers only spared Caesar's friend, Mark Antony, because they thought he was too lazy to cause them any trouble. Yet it was Antony who avenged Caesar and became the second important man in Cleopatra's life.

WHAT WAS MARK ANTONY LIKE?

Antony grew up during a brutal civil war. He became a wild young man who often got into trouble. When he was 25, he went to Greece to study public speaking and the arts of war. He was a natural soldier and after his first great success in Egypt he quickly became Caesar's right-hand man. The Romans expected their leaders to behave in a dignified way but Antony was a great lover of practical jokes, drinking parties and beautiful actresses. At the time of Caesar's death he had been married several times. His wife, Fulvia, was the widow of one of his friends.

Mark Antony was famously reckless. Here he drives his girlfriend through the streets of Rome in a chariot pulled by lions.

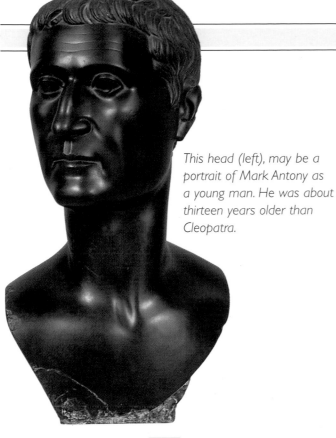

This head (left), may be a portrait of Mark Antony as a young man. He was about thirteen years older than Cleopatra.

Antony liked to play jokes on his serious wife, Fulvia, such as visiting his own house in disguise, pretending to be a messenger from himself. Another exploit he is famous for is driving a chariot drawn by lions through the streets of Rome!

WHO RULED ROME NEXT AFTER CAESAR?

At Caesar's funeral, Antony won over the Roman people with a great speech reminding them of Caesar's courage and generosity. He wanted to become the new leader of Rome, but Caesar's will had named his great-nephew, Octavian as his heir. Octavian was only 18 but he was clever and ruthless. Octavian won supporters by pretending he wanted to bring back the Republic. What he was really after was power for himself alone.

Coin of Octavian Caesar (right). He was Julius Caesar's great-nephew and adopted heir.

Coin showing Mark Antony's forceful wife, Fulvia, (left). She was the first wife of a Roman leader to play a really active role in politics.

WHAT HAPPENED TO CAESAR'S MURDERERS?

Antony and Octavian finally made a pact to rule the Roman world, together with a third man called Lepidus. Octavian was a poor general, but in 42 BC, Antony defeated Brutus and Cassius in two great battles at Philippi, in Greece. After their defeat, Brutus and Cassius killed themselves. Octavian returned to Rome while Antony became Roman overlord of the east.

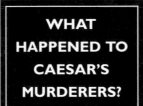

CLEOPATRA, THE LIVING GODDESS

Antony summoned all the rulers of the east to meet him at Tarsus and prove their loyalty to Rome. Cleopatra was the last to arrive. Shortly after her return from Rome, her half-brother Ptolemy 14 had died and Cleopatra's little son, Caesarion, had become her co-ruler under the name of Ptolemy 15.

Some people accused Cleopatra of poisoning her half-brother, but it was common in those days for children to die of sudden illnesses.

WHAT DID CLEOPATRA AND ANTONY WANT?

Now that Antony was almost as powerful as Caesar had been, Cleopatra wanted him as her husband. She might not have been the most beautiful woman in the world, but she was probably the richest. Antony needed money to pay for a war against the King of Parthia (in modern Iraq and Iran), who had been attacking the Roman province of Syria. He intended to impress Cleopatra with the power of Rome, but their meeting did not go as planned. When Cleopatra's ship reached Tarsus, the whole town rushed to see her. Antony was left all alone on his throne in the town square.

Gold pendant showing Aphrodite, the Greek goddess of love (left).

Statuette of the goddess Isis with her son, Horus, in her lap (right). In Egyptian mythology Isis had to brave many dangers to bring up Horus. Cleopatra was called 'the new Isis'.

Her ship had purple sails drenched in perfume and the crew were all beautiful girls. Cleopatra lay on a couch under a canopy of cloth of gold. She was dressed as the goddess Venus and surrounded by little boys playing Cupids. She refused to come ashore, but Antony and his officers were invited to her ship for dinner. The ship was brilliantly lit and the deck was knee-deep in rose petals. The Romans were dazzled by Cleopatra's wealth and charm.

After a wonderful dinner, Cleopatra told her guests that they could keep the magnificent furniture and the solid gold tableware they had been using!

Cleopatra welcomes Antony and his friends to a splendid dinner on board her ship.

He made her Rome's chief ally in the east and agreed to spend the winter with her in Alexandria. Cleopatra asked Antony to punish her sister, Arsinoe, who had been allowing people to call her queen. Antony had Arsinoe executed. Of Ptolemy's six children, Cleopatra was now the only one left.

CLEOPATRA'S FRIENDS

Most Romans despised foreigners, but Antony believed in following the customs of the country he was staying in. To please Cleopatra, he visited the local temples and went to debates at the Museum (*university*). She knew that he hated to be serious all the time, so she formed a group of friends called 'The Incomparable Livers'. They met nearly every night to hold parties in honour of Dionysus, the god of wine and ecstasy. The friends included writers, musicians and actors, as well as soldiers and politicians. Their aim was to live life to the full.

WHAT DID GUESTS EAT AND DRINK AT HER PARTIES?

Greek wines were usually drunk mixed with water and flavoured with honey and spices. The favourite meats at Greek feasts were pork and lamb. They were often cooked with spices like cummin, coriander and poppy seeds. Mullet, catfish and eels were popular for the fish course and all kinds of wild birds were eaten. Whole roast pig stuffed with thrushes might be served. For dessert there would be nuts, fruit such as figs, grapes and pomegranates, and cakes soaked in honey.

Antony and Cleopatra and their friends enjoy a splendid dinner in honour of the god Dionysus.

At Cleopatra's parties everything had to be perfectly cooked. For a party of twelve people, eight wild boars were cooked at different speeds, so that whatever time Antony wanted to eat, there would always be a perfect roast ready!

Sometimes at night, Antony and Cleopatra would disguise themselves as servants and wander round the city to mix with ordinary people.

DID ANTONY GET BORED LIVING WITH CLEOPATRA?

No. She also took him hunting and fishing. Once when he had had no luck on a fishing trip, he bribed a fisherman to swim underwater and attach live fish to his line. Cleopatra guessed what had happened. The next time they went fishing, she got one of her servants to fix a piece of salted fish to Antony's line. Everyone laughed when Antony pulled in his catch.

Mosaic with a head of Dionysus, the Greek god of wine and ecstasy (left). Mark Antony was known as the 'new Dionysus'.

Copper fish hooks used for catching Nile fish in ancient times (right).

DID ANTONY PLAN TO STAY WITH CLEOPATRA?

In the spring, he set out for Syria, where the Parthians had been causing trouble. Cleopatra was now expecting his child. She hoped to see him again in a few months, but news from Italy that his wife, Fulvia, and his younger brother, Lucius, had started a revolt against Octavian forced him to change his plans.

Silver cup of the kind that Antony and Cleopatra would have drunk from at their dinner parties. The decoration shows the followers of Dionysus riding wild beasts.

THE PRICE OF PEACE

Octavian had been taking away people's farms to give to his soldiers. This made him very unpopular in Italy. But the war in Italy also started because Antony's wife, Fulvia, had a personal grudge against Octavian. He had agreed to marry her daughter but had broken his word. Fulvia was fiercely loyal to Antony, but their marriage was a stormy one. Some people said that she only started the war to get Antony away from Cleopatra. Fulvia was soon defeated by Octavian's troops and forced to flee to Greece.

WOULD ANTONY GO TO WAR WITH OCTAVIAN?

He was very angry with Fulvia for starting the war but he was ready to fight Octavian. He was joined by a large fleet led by a friend called Ahenobarbus. There was some fighting, but the ordinary soldiers on both sides made it clear that they didn't want another civil war. In the meantime, Fulvia died. It was said she died of a broken heart.

Gold and carnelian ring (left), with head of Octavia, the only sister of Octavian.

HOW DID ANTONY AND OCTAVIAN MAKE PEACE?

The two men felt that they couldn't trust each other unless they were related by marriage. Antony agreed to marry Octavian's sister, Octavia. She was a recent widow with three children. Antony's marriage made everyone in Italy very happy, but it must have been a severe blow to Cleopatra. A few weeks later she gave birth to twins. The children were called Cleopatra and Alexander.

Carving of the dwarf god, Bes, at an Egyptian temple (above). The Egyptians believed that he helped women to give birth and protected young children. Cleopatra was not to see her twins' father again for over 3 years.

Having sent his wife Octavia back to Rome, Antony and his fleet (right) sailed east to join Cleopatra in Syria.

*A*ntony and Octavia had two daughters, they were both called Antonia. Roman noblewomen were always known by the female form of their father's surname. The elder Antonia was to become the grandmother of the Emperor Nero, while the younger was the grandmother of the Emperor Caligula and mother of the Emperor Claudius.

WAS ANTONY HAPPY WITH OCTAVIA?

*O*ctavia tried to be a loyal wife, but because she was Octavian's sister, Antony could never quite trust her. He was becoming increasingly angry with Octavian for not keeping his promises. Octavian failed to send Antony any troops to fight the Parthians because he didn't want Antony to have a great victory. Antony determined to defeat Parthia without Octavian's help. He sent Octavia and the children back to Rome and sailed east.

Coins (left), issued to celebrate the marriage of Antony and Octavia.

DISASTER IN PARTHIA

As soon as he arrived in the east, Antony asked Cleopatra to meet him in Antioch. If he could conquer Parthia, he would become master of the Roman world, but he needed Cleopatra's help.

DID CLEOPATRA FORGIVE ANTONY?

As a woman, she may have felt bitter about Antony deserting her. As a leader, she had to put her feelings aside and think of her country. Some hard bargaining probably went on in Antioch. Cleopatra agreed to provide money and ships for Antony's Parthian campaign. In return, he gave her nearly all the countries that had once been part of the Ptolemies' empire. He may also have gone through some kind of marriage ceremony with her. Cleopatra returned home in triumph. She had kept Egypt independent and got back its lost empire.

This head may be a portrait of Cleopatra in her thirties, at around the time she gave birth to her fourth child.

Coin of the Parthian King, Phraates IV, whose soldiers defeated Antony.

HOW DID ANTONY PLAN TO ATTACK PARTHIA?

Earlier Roman generals had been defeated in the hot plains of south Parthia. Antony decided to attack from the north across the mountains. On the march northwards he had to leave behind the slower wagons carrying vital food supplies and siege equipment with troops from Armenia to guard them. Just when he needed his siege equipment to capture the Parthians' regional capital, Phraaspa, and make it his base for a long campaign, the Armenians deserted to the enemy. Nearly all Antony's wagons were captured. Winter was near and the Romans were running out of food. Full of despair, Antony gave his army the order to retreat to Syria.

DID HE GET HIS ARMY HOME?

Yes. After much hardship and many battles they finally reached the Parthian border. There, the Parthians who had been following Antony's army, unstrung their bows to show that they wouldn't attack again. They saluted the Romans for their courage. Antony's army still faced a long march through the snows of Armenia. By the time he reached Syria again, he had lost over 30,000 of his original army of 100,000 men.

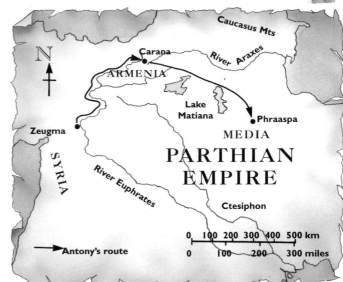

Antony's plan to attack Parthia from the north was unsuccessful (above).

Antony's army were good soldiers, but the Parthians had more horsemen and archers; they would shoot at the Romans from a distance and then ride away.

QUEEN OF KINGS

Antony sent a message to Cleopatra, asking her to come as quickly as she could with money and supplies for his exhausted army. His wife, Octavia, also set out to bring Antony soldiers and ships.

This head is thought to be a portrait of Octavia, Cleopatra's rival.

WHO WOULD ANTONY CHOOSE?

After his defeat it was Cleopatra he longed to see. If she was slow in coming she had a good excuse. At the age of 36 she had just given birth to her third child by Antony, called Ptolemy Philadelphos. Once they were reunited, Cleopatra begged Antony never to desert her again. Antony sent Octavia a letter telling her to go back to Rome. Politics had brought Antony and Cleopatra together, but they had come to love each other.

WHAT DID ANTONY DO NEXT?

He went back with Cleopatra to Alexandria. This was probably the first time he had met his three children by Cleopatra. Antony's luck soon changed for the better. He won a war against the treacherous king of Armenia and chose to celebrate his victory in Alexandria. This offended people in Rome, but what he gave Cleopatra at a splendid ceremony in the Gymnasium, the largest building in Alexandria, upset them even more.

WHAT DID HE GIVE CLEOPATRA?

Antony made a speech proclaiming Caesarion the true son and heir of Julius Caesar. He gave him the new title of 'King of Kings'. Antony and Cleopatra's three children were all made kings and queens of Armenia, Parthia, Cyrenaica (modern Libya) and most of Asia Minor (modern Turkey and Syria). To show that Cleopatra would be the supreme ruler of this new empire, she was given the title 'Queen of Kings and Queen of her sons who are Kings'.

Silver coin of Cleopatra, giving her the title 'Queen of Kings'. This must have confirmed the worst fears of Romans about the part Antony intended her to play in his empire.

Antony declares Cleopatra 'Queen of Kings' and gives kingdoms to her four children.

DID CLEOPATRA WANT TO RULE THE WORLD?

Alexander the Great had tried to unite the races of the world under Greek leadership. Cleopatra hoped to rebuild his empire. Octavian also wanted to be sole ruler of a world empire, so war between Rome and Egypt was inevitable.

Silver coin of Antony (right), showing him as overlord of the Near East.

THE ENEMY OF ROME

Octavian claimed that Cleopatra's plan was to become queen of Rome. He spread all sorts of gossip about her. She was accused of being an unfaithful wife and a bad ruler, who gave too much power to servants, such as her maid Charmian, and her hairdresser, Iras. She was said to have bewitched Antony and turned him into a helpless drunkard.

WAS ANTONY BEWITCHED BY CLEOPATRA?

Some of the stories about Antony's passion for Cleopatra may be true. He is said to have read love letters from her in the middle of judging court cases and he shocked Roman friends by giving her a foot massage during a banquet. Most Romans did not approve of men being affectionate in public and they admired people with a simple lifestyle. Cleopatra was accused of living a life of wicked luxury, and even of drinking pearls.

Gold buckle set with garnets. Cleopatra's Egypt was seen by Octavian as a rich source of treasure to pay his troops.

Cleopatra drinks a pearl dissolved in vinegar to win a bet with Antony.

DID CLEOPATRA REALLY DRINK PEARLS?

Cleopatra wore the two largest pearls in the world set into earrings. She is said to have bet Antony that she could spend 10,000,000 sesterces, (around half a million pounds), on a single dinner. Cleopatra gave Antony and his friends a lavish meal, but he mocked her for its cheapness. Then Cleopatra called for a cup of vinegar. She dropped one of the fabulously valuable earrings into the cup. When the vinegar had dissolved the pearl, Cleopatra drank it. She would have destroyed the other earring too, but everyone agreed that Cleopatra had won her bet.

THE STORY OF THE PEARL IN VINEGAR

Vinegar is not strong enough to instantly dissolve a pearl. Any acid that is, would have been fatal to drink. Either Cleopatra was playing a trick on Antony, or the story just isn't true. Most of these stories were written by her enemies.

Cleopatra was seen by the Romans as representing everything exotic and dangerous. She was said to have enslaved Antony just as Omphale enslaved Hercules in Greek mythology. In fact, Cleopatra seems to have been a good ruler and a faithful wife, and Antony had been fond of wild drinking parties long before he lived with Cleopatra.

Pearl and gold earrings of a type that Cleopatra might have worn (above). She was famous for her love of pearls. The Roman poet, Lucan, describes her attending a banquet loaded with these 'spoils of the Red Sea'.

WOULD THERE BE WAR BETWEEN ROME AND EGYPT?

Octavian claimed Antony was no longer loyal to Rome because he was under Cleopatra's spell. In 32 BC Octavian seized sole power in Italy. Many leading Romans left to join Antony. A few months later, Octavian had Cleopatra named an official 'Enemy of Rome' and declared war on Egypt.

Silver dish thought to show Cleopatra as Africa (left). She is wearing an elephant headdress and is surrounded by wild animals. To the Romans she represented everything exotic and dangerous.

BATTLE AT SEA

Antony and Cleopatra spent the winter at Ephesus and then sailed for Greece. Their huge fleet was paid for by Cleopatra and she was present at all Antony's councils of war. To make it clear that she was his wife, he sent divorce papers to Octavia.

Carving of one of the Roman warships that defeated the Egyptians at Actium (left).

Some of the money used to pay Antony's troops. This coin (above), shows one of Antony's warships.

HOW DID THE WAR GO?

If Antony had attacked Octavian in Italy straightaway, he might have won, but he didn't want to invade his own country. Octavian had a brilliant admiral called Agrippa. After some months of fighting, Agrippa trapped Antony's fleet inside the harbour at Actium (in modern Greece). Octavian had landed his army in the hills north of Actium, but he refused to come down and fight Antony. Antony's supply routes were cut off. His army ran short of food and fever spread through his camp. Many of his allies went over to Octavian.

WHAT CHOICES DID ANTONY HAVE?

His officers wanted him to force a land battle with Octavian. But Antony decided it was more important to preserve his fleet and all the gold that Cleopatra had with her to pay for the war. He put Cleopatra and her treasure on his flagship, guarded by 60 Egyptian ships. On a stormy autumn day, Antony used the rest of his ships to try to break through Agrippa's fleet. In the middle of the battle, all the Egyptian ships suddenly sailed away, leaving Antony's fleet outnumbered.

Portrait of Agrippa (left). This brilliant admiral later married Octavian's only daughter.

Antony's ships (below), try to break through Agrippa's fleet in the Bay of Actium.

DID CLEOPATRA BETRAY ANTONY?

Cleopatra was famous for her courage, so it is more likely that she was obeying an order from Antony to get the Egyptian fleet away. As soon as Cleopatra's ships were clear of Agrippa's fleet, Antony changed to a fast ship to follow her. He may have hoped that the rest of his fleet could escape too, but they were surrounded by Agrippa's ships. Agrippa used fireballs and thousands of Antony's men were burned to death or drowned. When Antony rejoined his flagship he was too upset to speak to anyone for three days.

THE FATE OF ANTONY

Antony and Cleopatra still had their treasure and most of their fleet, but the land army they had left at Actium was bribed into fighting for Octavian. Cleopatra faced the situation with her usual courage and energy but Antony sank into a deep depression. Cleopatra ordered the fleet to hang out garlands to pretend they were coming home victorious. She wanted to be firmly back in charge before people realized they were beaten.

HOW DID ANTONY AND CLEOPATRA FACE DEFEAT?

As Octavian got closer to Egypt, they tried to make peace with him. Antony even offered to kill himself if Octavian would spare Cleopatra and the children, but Octavian refused all his offers. Cleopatra sent Caesarion to southern Egypt to keep him safe from Octavian. She entertained her friends more lavishly than ever. When Octavian's army was close to Alexandria, Antony finally roused himself and made a successful attack on their advance guard. He rushed back to the palace to celebrate with Cleopatra.

Bronze head from a statue of Octavian that once stood at Egypt's southern frontier.

The skeletons on this silver cup (left), were to remind the drinker to enjoy life while he could because death might be close.

Coin showing Antony in his last years (left). He was a natural leader, but in the end his luck deserted him.

WAS CLEOPATRA DEAD?

As he lay in agony, Antony learned that Cleopatra was still alive. He was carried to her locked tomb. She opened a window and, with the help of her servants Iras and Charmian, pulled Antony up into the tomb. Cleopatra was half mad with grief, but Antony called for one last cup of wine. He begged Cleopatra to think of her own safety and died in her arms.

Antony stabs himself, after his servant refuses to kill him.

WHY DID ANTONY KILL HIMSELF?

The next day Antony tried to rally the city, but most of the Egyptian army surrendered to Octavian. In his despair, Antony accused Cleopatra of betraying him. She and her servants had taken refuge inside the tomb that had been built for her close to the palace. Antony heard a rumour that Cleopatra was already dead. Desperate to join her, he asked one of his servants to kill him. The man could not bear to hurt him and killed himself instead. Antony then stabbed himself in the stomach.

THE DEATH OF CLEOPATRA

Octavian was now master of Alexandria, but he was anxious to get hold of Cleopatra's treasure to reward his supporters.

HOW WAS CLEOPATRA TAKEN PRISONER?

Cleopatra's gold, silver, emeralds, pearls, ivory, ebony and precious spices were stored in her tomb, surrounded by firewood. Octavian was afraid that she would burn the treasure, so he sent two officers to pretend to negotiate with her. While one stood talking outside the tomb, the other climbed in through a window and grabbed her. She tried to stab herself, but the officer got the dagger away from her.

DID CLEOPATRA AND OCTAVIAN MEET?

For the sake of her children and her country, Cleopatra had to try and win Octavian over. She was nearly forty, but still very attractive. When Octavian visited she read out some of the letters that Julius Caesar had written to her and told him how like Caesar he was. Octavian promised to treat her well, but soon after, she was warned that he planned to take her back to Rome to walk in chains at his Triumph. Cleopatra decided to kill herself.

Cleopatra and her faithful servants, Iras and Charmian, choose to die together rather than be taken to Rome.

HOW DID CLEOPATRA KILL HERSELF?

On the night she planned to die, Cleopatra kissed the urn holding Antony's ashes and garlanded it with flowers. She took a bath and enjoyed her last meal. She sent a sealed letter to Octavian, asking him to bury her beside Antony. Then Iras and Charmian helped Cleopatra to dress in her best royal robes. She calmly took some poison and lay down on a golden couch to die. Iras and Charmian chose to die with their beloved queen.

CLEOPATRA'S DEATH

Some ancient writers say that she pricked herself with a poisoned hair-pin; others that she let herself be bitten by a poisonous snake called an asp. If she used snake venom, it probably came from a cobra, which was a royal symbol in Egypt.

Cleopatra's burial place has never been found, but her coffin would probably have looked like this one (above). The dead woman is dressed like the goddess Isis and holds a wreath of roses.

Snake bracelet in gold (left). The snake was a symbol of Isis. Images of Cleopatra's body wearing snake bracelets may have led to the story that she was killed by a poisonous snake.

HOW DID OCTAVIAN REACT TO HER DEATH?

Octavian is said to have sent for snake-charmers to try and suck out the poison. Secretly, he was probably relieved that Cleopatra was dead. He praised her courage and honoured her wish to be buried beside Antony. Statues of Charmian and Iras were set up outside Cleopatra's tomb, so that everyone would remember the queen's faithful servants.

CLEOPATRA AND ANTONY'S CHILDREN

Octavian had Antony's eldest son by Fulvia, fourteen year old Antyllus, dragged from sanctuary and beheaded. When Cleopatra's son, sixteen year old Caesarion was tricked into surrendering, he was murdered too. With the death of Caesarion, Julius Caesar's son by Cleopatra, Octavian was now Caesar's only heir.

WAS OCTAVIAN NOW ALL POWERFUL?

When he returned to Rome he celebrated a Triumph over Egypt. Antony and Cleopatra's three children were forced to walk in chains behind a painted image of the dead queen, but their lives were spared, probably at the request of Octavia. Octavian was not content to be an elected Dictator like his great-uncle, Caesar. In 27 BC he became the first Emperor of Rome under the name of Augustus Caesar.

As Emperor of Rome, Octavian changed his name to Augustus Caesar, meaning 'revered' Caesar in Latin. To commemorate his greatest victory, Augustus changed the name of the month in which Cleopatra had died from Sextilis to August.

Coin issued by Octavian to mark his victory over Egypt (above). The Nile crocodile was a symbol of Egypt.

Jewelled cameo (right), showing Octavian after he became Emperor of Rome under the name of Augustus.

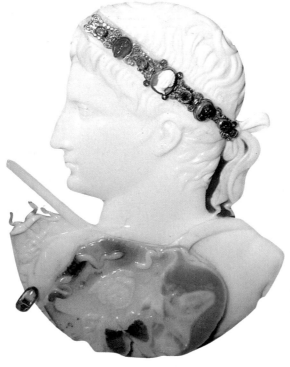

Greeks and Egyptians worship a statue of Cleopatra after her death.

This beautiful carving may be a portrait of Antony and Octavia's daughter, Antonia the younger. Her son, Emperor Claudius, made Britain part of the Roman Empire.

WHAT HAPPENED TO ANTONY AND CLEOPATRA'S CHILDREN?

Octavia generously brought up all Antony's children as if they were her own. Later on Antony and Cleopatra's daughter, Princess Cleopatra Selene, married the young king of Mauretania, (Morocco), and her two brothers were allowed to go and live with her there.

HOW WAS CLEOPATRA REMEMBERED?

The Romans saw Cleopatra as the 'serpent of the Nile'. To the Egyptians, she was a great ruler and patriot. Egypt was now just a province of Rome, but Cleopatra was worshipped as a form of the goddess Isis long after her death. Even when Egypt became a Christian country, Cleopatra's memory was still honoured. An Egyptian bishop wrote that Cleopatra 'was the most noble and wise of women, great in herself and in her achievements.'

70 BC	65 BC	60 BC	55 BC	50 BC

58 BC
PTOLEMY 12
FORCED TO FLEE
TO ROME.

69 BC?
BIRTH OF
CLEOPATRA 7,
DAUGHTER OF
PTOLEMY 12.

55 BC
PTOLEMY 12
RESTORED TO THE
THRONE WITH HELP
FROM ANTONY.

CLEOPATRA 7 KEY DATES

51 BC
DEATH OF PTOLEMY 12.
CLEOPATRA 7 AND HER
BROTHER PTOLEMY 13
BECOME RULERS OF EGYPT.

IMPORTANT DATES BEFORE 69 BC

3,100 BC
Egypt united by the first Pharaohs.

510 BC
Founding of the Roman Republic.

343 BC
Last Egyptian Pharaoh defeated by the Persians.

332 BC
Alexander the Great of Macedonia conquers
Egypt and founds Alexandria.

305 BC
General Ptolemy founds
a dynasty of Macedonian rulers of Egypt.

102 BC?
Birth of Julius Caesar.

83 BC
Birth of Mark Antony.

80 BC
Ptolemy 12, becomes king of Egypt.

IMPORTANT DATES AFTER 30 BC

27 BC
Octavian becomes Augustus Caesar,
the first Emperor of Rome.

25 BC
Cleopatra's daughter, Cleopatra Selene, marries
the King of Mauretania.

40 AD
Their son, Ptolemy, is murdered
by his cousin, the Emperor Caligula.

41 AD
Antony's grandson Claudius
becomes Emperor of Rome.

323 AD
Egypt becomes a Christian country.

641 AD
Egypt conquered by the Arabs.

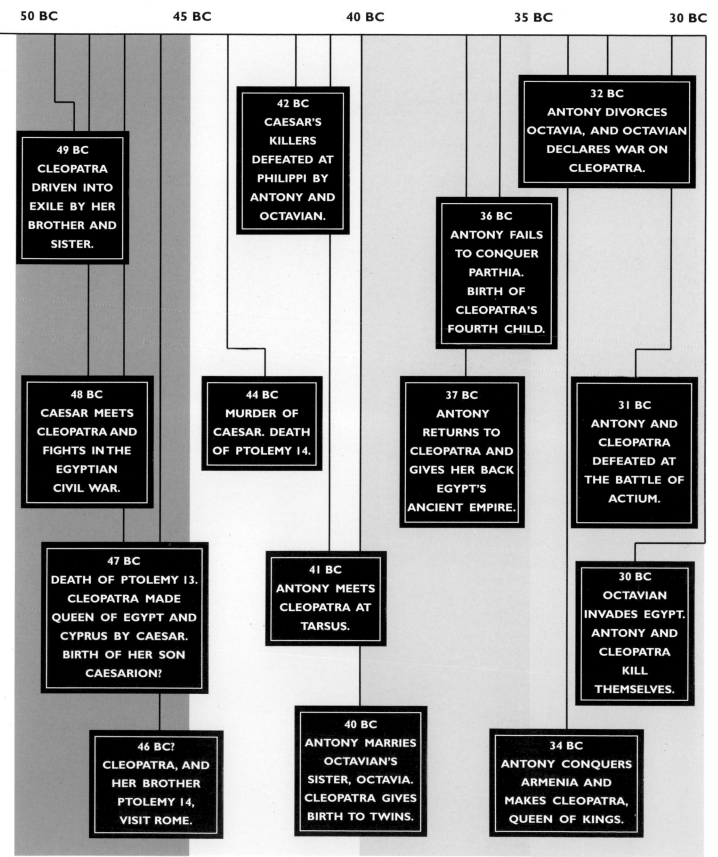

50 BC　　　　**45 BC**　　　　**40 BC**　　　　**35 BC**　　　　**30 BC**

49 BC
CLEOPATRA DRIVEN INTO EXILE BY HER BROTHER AND SISTER.

48 BC
CAESAR MEETS CLEOPATRA AND FIGHTS IN THE EGYPTIAN CIVIL WAR.

47 BC
DEATH OF PTOLEMY 13. CLEOPATRA MADE QUEEN OF EGYPT AND CYPRUS BY CAESAR. BIRTH OF HER SON CAESARION?

46 BC?
CLEOPATRA, AND HER BROTHER PTOLEMY 14, VISIT ROME.

44 BC
MURDER OF CAESAR. DEATH OF PTOLEMY 14.

42 BC
CAESAR'S KILLERS DEFEATED AT PHILIPPI BY ANTONY AND OCTAVIAN.

41 BC
ANTONY MEETS CLEOPATRA AT TARSUS.

40 BC
ANTONY MARRIES OCTAVIAN'S SISTER, OCTAVIA. CLEOPATRA GIVES BIRTH TO TWINS.

37 BC
ANTONY RETURNS TO CLEOPATRA AND GIVES HER BACK EGYPT'S ANCIENT EMPIRE.

36 BC
ANTONY FAILS TO CONQUER PARTHIA. BIRTH OF CLEOPATRA'S FOURTH CHILD.

34 BC
ANTONY CONQUERS ARMENIA AND MAKES CLEOPATRA, QUEEN OF KINGS.

32 BC
ANTONY DIVORCES OCTAVIA, AND OCTAVIAN DECLARES WAR ON CLEOPATRA.

31 BC
ANTONY AND CLEOPATRA DEFEATED AT THE BATTLE OF ACTIUM.

30 BC
OCTAVIAN INVADES EGYPT. ANTONY AND CLEOPATRA KILL THEMSELVES.

GLOSSARY

ASP A poisonous snake, probably a cobra. Cleopatra may have died from an asp bite.

CUPID Roman god of love. Shown as a little boy with wings.

DICTATOR Title used by Roman generals who were given supreme power in times of emergency.

DIONYSUS Greek god of wine and ecstasy.

GYMNASIUM A large building used for public meetings as well as sports.

HENNA Red-brown dye made from the leaves of the henna bush. Used to colour hair or nails.

ISIS Egyptian goddess of motherhood and magic. She was the widow of Osiris and the mother of the hawk god, Horus.

KOHL Glittering black powder mixed with water or fat for use as eye make-up.

MALACHITE Green mineral ground into powder and used in eye make-up.

MUSEUM A temple of the Nine Muses where writers and thinkers could work and study.

OCHRE Red or yellow pigment made from clay. Sometimes used to colour the cheeks or lips.

OSIRIS Egyptian god of the dead and of the harvest.

PARTHIANS Tribes from what is now Iran, who were famous horsemen and archers.

PHARAOH Title of the ruler of Egypt. The word means 'Great House' in Egyptian.

PHAROS The great lighthouse at Alexandria. One of the Seven Wonders of the ancient world.

PLUTARCH A Greek author who wrote biographies of Julius Caesar and Mark Antony.

PTOLEMIES The line of Greek kings and queens who ruled Egypt from 305 to 30 BC. All the kings were called Ptolemy (pronounced Tolerme).

ROMAN REPUBLIC A system where the heads of families elected the men who would govern Rome.

SEXTILIS One of the months of the Roman year. Re-named August after the Emperor Augustus.

TRIUMPH A parade held to celebrate the return to Rome of a victorious general.

VENUS The Roman goddess of love and beauty. The Greeks had a similar goddess called APHRODITE.

INDEX

EGYPT AND THE ROMAN PROVINCES AT THE ACCESSION OF CLEOPATRA AS QUEEN OF EGYPT, 51 BC